Perfect the present moment, perfect moments will become a perfect minute, hour, day, month, year and life.

Even if you are born with luck and skill, you are incomplete without hard work and experience.

Have a method for life. People who have changed the world even had a method for their madness.

Enlightenment is knowing the reason behind everything.

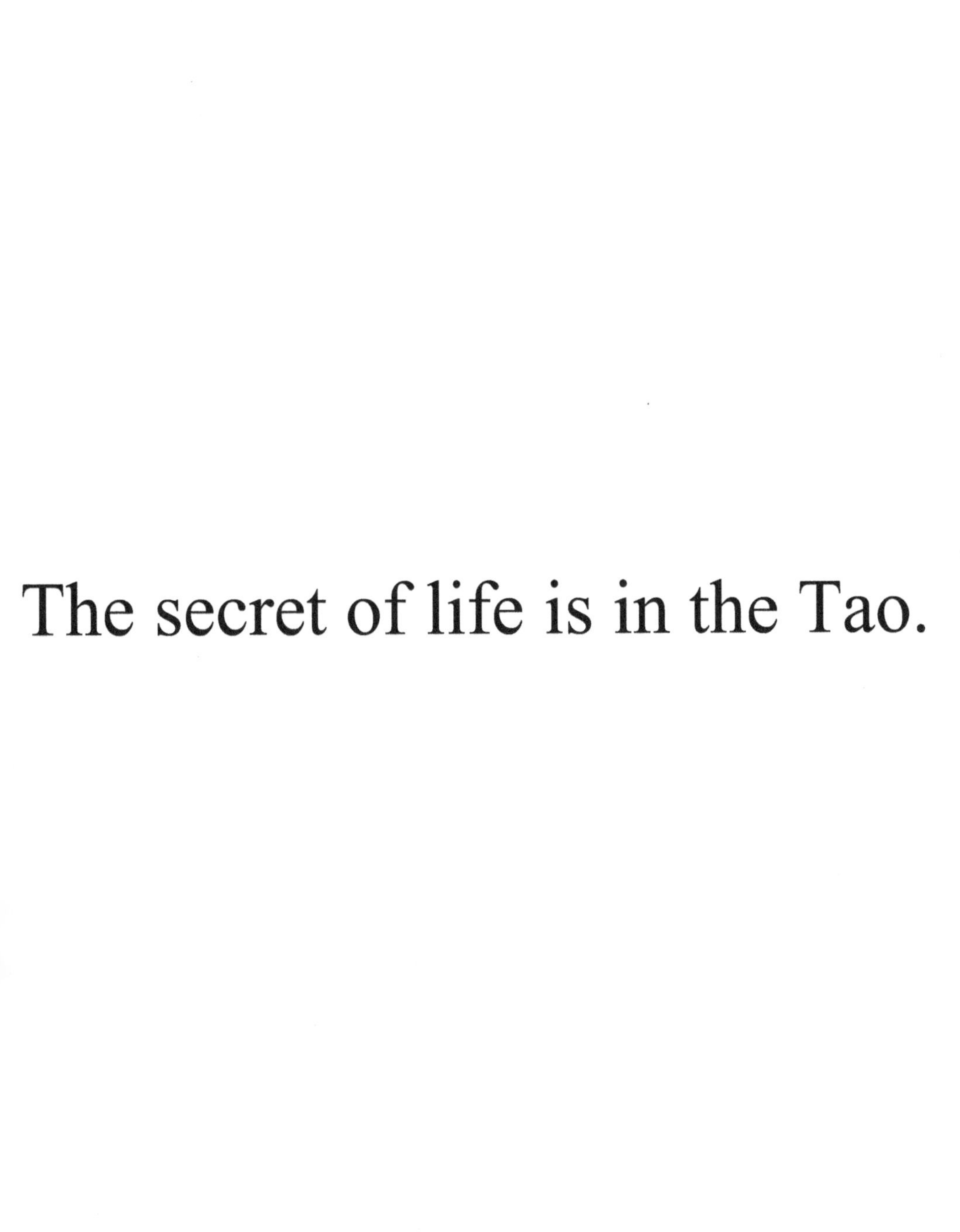

The secret of life is in the Tao.

The world is made up of both magic and reality.

We know light because there is darkness and we know darkness because there is light.

Humans are omnivores. Between good and evil is human survival.

The masculine is cold but wise. The feminine is warm but can get overwhelmed by emotions.

Strong relationships are made with a combination of love and similarities.

Practice yoga, live the middle path, read the tao te ching, eat halal and destroy the inner sinner gradually.

Do not believe blindly in everything. A spiritual person should have a balance between faith and wisdom.

Thoughtlessness will take you higher. Mindfulness will ground you. The pure can withstand.

Good health is not found in a magic pill. It is found in food, exercise, sleep, air and sunlight.

Look up at the stars, what and where. They will tell you a part of your life story. The rest is your wisdom of the world.

A midlife crisis is common in the early thirties.

We are all fools till the end. A fool who does not know he is a fool is a greater fool than a fool who knows that he is a fool.

Every arrogant action of man has an equal and opposite reaction that man is ignorant about.

We can save nature. Plant a tree.

We all have experiences that
may be helpful to another.
Write a book.

Give a man something and he will use it for a day, teach a man something and he will use it for a lifetime.

Learn everything you can.
Knowledge and experience in
something can help you in
another.

Live a balanced life. Great success in one aspect of life may mean failure in another.

War between nations or races is ignorance. War between good and evil makes sense.

Doing nothing in front of evil will make the world a worse place for you and your child to live in.